Dinosaur Discovery

BRACHIOSAURUS

NICKI CLAUSEN-GRACE

Black Rabbit Books

Bolt is published by Black Rabbit Books
P.O. Box 227, Mankato, Minnesota, 56002.
www.blackrabbitbooks.com
Copyright © 2025 Black Rabbit Books

Alissa Thielges, editor; Rhea Magaro, designer and photo researcher

All rights reserved. No part of this book may be reproduced, stored in a retrieval system or transmitted in any form or by any means, electronic, mechanical, photocopying, recording, or otherwise, without written permission from the publisher.

Library of Congress Cataloging-in-Publication Data
Names: Clausen-Grace, Nicki, author.
Title: Brachiosaurus / Nicki Clausen-Grace.
Description: Mankato, Minnesota: Black Rabbit Books, [2024] | Series: Dinosaur discovery | Includes bibliographical references and index. | Audience: Ages 8–12 | Audience: Grades 4–6 | Summary: "One of the most famous long-necked dinosaurs, Brachiosaurus was once a huge, slow-moving plant-eater. Reluctant readers discover what life was like for this Jurassic dinosaur through diagrams, graphs, powerful illustrations, and fun text" —Provided by publisher.
Identifiers: LCCN 2023035668 (print) | LCCN 2023035669 (ebook) | ISBN 9781623105891 (library binding) | ISBN 9781623105952 (ebook)
Subjects: LCSH: Brachiosaurus—Juvenile literature.
Classification: LCC QE862.S3 C523 2024 (print) | LCC QE862.S3 (ebook) | DDC 567.913—dc23/eng/20231017
LC record available at https://lccn.loc.gov/2023035668
LC ebook record available at https://lccn.loc.gov/2023035669

Printed in China.

Image Credits

Alamy: Aleksandrs Tihonovs 26–27, Dan Leeth 29 (b); Getty: De Agostini Picture Library cover; Matt Wedel 16–17; The Field Museum in Chicago 17; Science Source: Album / Prisma 29 (t), James Kuether 14–15, Phil Wilson/Stocktrek Images 4–5, Richard Bizley 22, Stocktrek Images 9; Shutterstock: Art studio G 25 (b), Dotted Yeti 1, 12–13, 31, Elenarts 3, Hedzun Vasyl 18–19 (bkgd), Herschel Hoffmeyer 24, Irina Boldina 21 (m), Jomic 25 (t), Kozyreva Elena 25 (blue), Leriaphoto 21 (t), MERCURY studio 21 (b), Michael Rosskothen 6, Orla 32, Ton Bangkeaw 8–9, Warpaint 10–11, Zhenyakot 25 (Allosaurus); Wikipedia Commons: 27 (inset)
Every effort has been made to contact copyright holders for material reproduced in this book. Any omissions will be rectified in subsequent printings if notice is given to the publisher.

CONTENTS

CHAPTER 1
Meet the
Brachiosaurus......4

CHAPTER 2
Where and When
They Lived.........12

CHAPTER 3
What They Ate.....20

CHAPTER 4
New Discoveries....27

Other Resources...........30

CHAPTER 1

Meet the BRACHIOSAURUS

A small dinosaur hides in the shade of a mountain. The mountain slowly moves. It isn't really a mountain. It is the giant leg of a Brachiosaurus. The little dinosaur speeds away. The Brachiosaurus moves to get fresh plants. Each step shakes the earth.

Giant Giraffe?

Brachiosaurus stretches its neck up. That's where the tastiest leaves are. It pushes up with long front legs, reaching even higher. Brachiosaurus closes its mouth over a branch. Its small head pulls back. This **strips** all the leaves from the branch.

> Brachiosaurus means "arm reptile." It got the name because its front legs were longer than its back legs.

On the Move

Brachiosaurus probably lived in groups called **herds**. It was a huge dinosaur. It took a lot of energy to move. That is why it moved slowly. It also didn't go very far. Brachiosaurus ate all the plants in an area. It would only move when the trees were bare. It stayed away from hills. Walking uphill was more difficult.

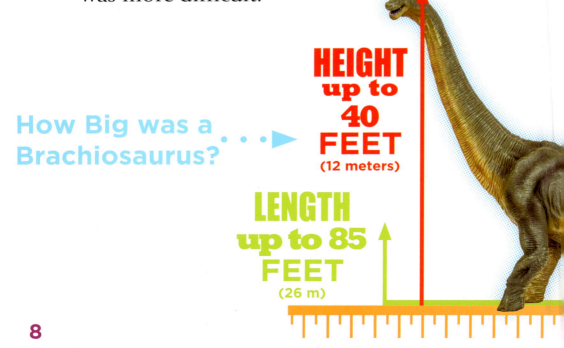

How Big was a Brachiosaurus?

HEIGHT up to 40 FEET (12 meters)

LENGTH up to 85 FEET (26 m)

BRACHIOSAURUS FEATURES

SMALL HEAD

TALL NECK

TAIL

CHAPTER 2

Where and WHEN THEY LIVED

Brachiosaurus lived in the late Jurassic period. This was 154 to 150 million years ago. It lived on flat land. Sometimes the weather was wet. Sometimes it was very dry. There were plenty of plants and trees then. Low palm trees and **ferns** covered the ground. Pine trees grew cones. Horsetails looked like bamboo with bushy tops.

WHEN THEY LIVED

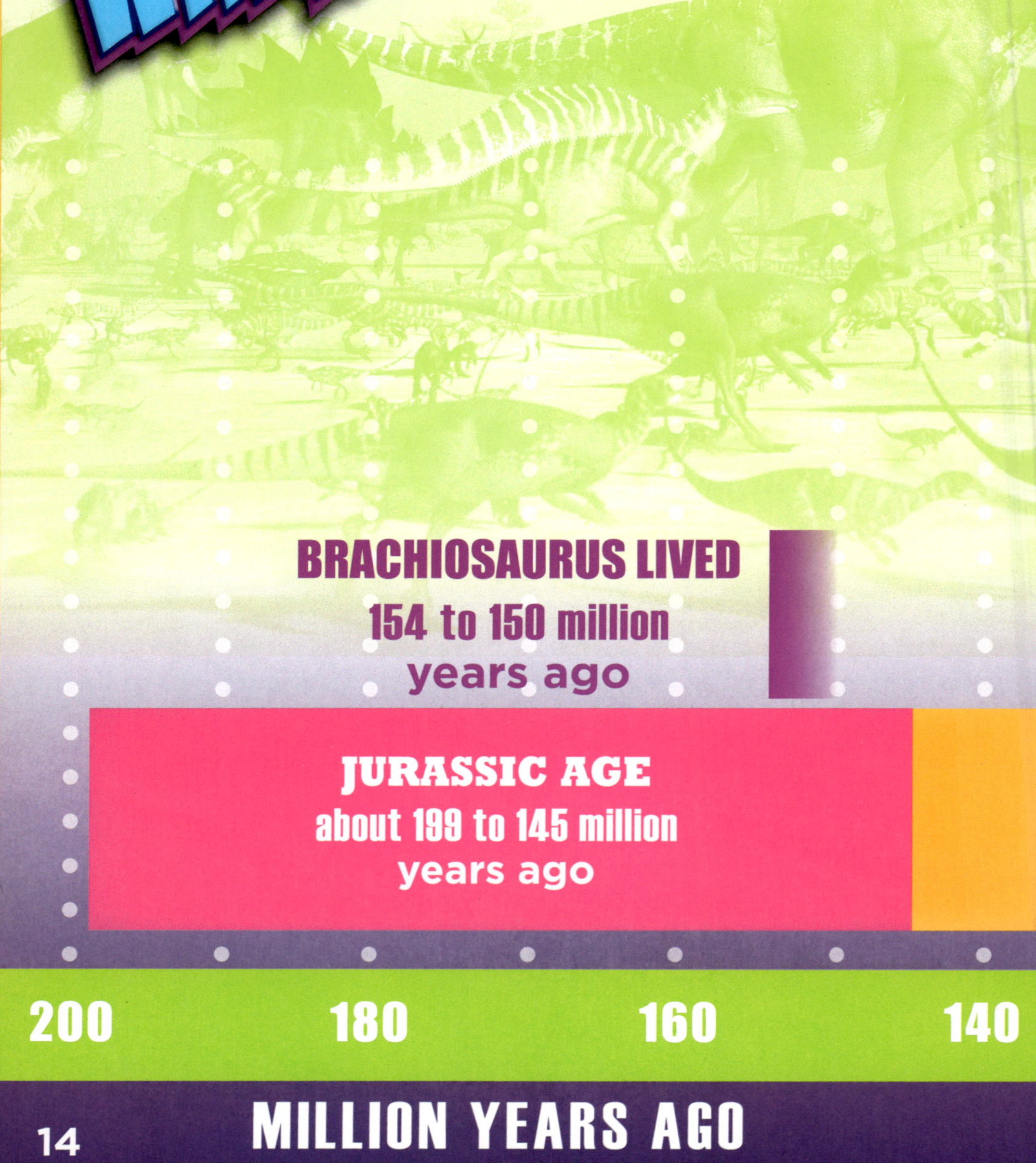

BRACHIOSAURUS LIVED
154 to 150 million
years ago

JURASSIC AGE
about 199 to 145 million
years ago

200   180   160   140

MILLION YEARS AGO

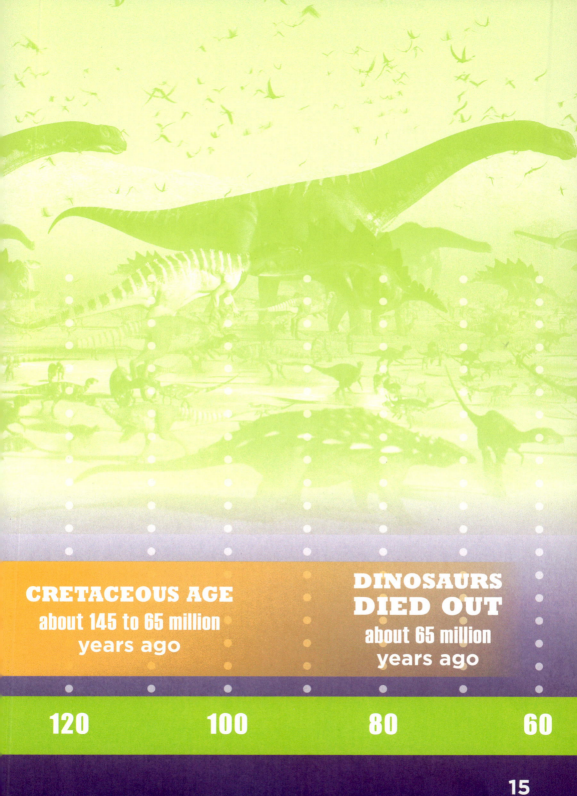

CRETACEOUS AGE
about 145 to 65 million years ago

DINOSAURS DIED OUT
about 65 million years ago

120   100   80   60

A Big Discovery

It can take a long time to figure out each type of dinosaur from **fossils**. The first Brachiosaurus fossil was found in 1883. It was a skull. A museum thought it was Apatosaurus. They didn't know it was Brachiosaurus until 1998. Then, in 1900, more fossils were discovered. They were in Colorado. People named the remains Brachiosaurus in 1903.

WHERE BRACHIOSAURUS FOSSILS HAVE BEEN FOUND

CHAPTER 3

Brachiosaurus was a plant eater. It ate pine trees, tree ferns, **ginkgoes** and **cycads**. Its long neck reached high. It ate from tall trees. Strong jaws and spoon-shaped teeth scraped leaves off. It swallowed leaves and stems whole. It still needed help to break apart tough leaves, though. It swallowed rocks along with plants. These rocks ground up the plants in its stomach.

Some of the Plants Brachiosaurus Ate

tree ferns

ginkgoes

cycads

Big Meals

It took a lot of food to power the gigantic Brachiosaurus. It spent most of its time eating. It had to eat about 880 pounds (400 kilograms) each day to live. It didn't have to **compete** with other types of dinosaurs for food. Other plant eaters ate leaves close to the ground.

Watch Out!

Brachiosaurus ate a lot. But not many things ate it. Adults were so big that meat eaters left them alone. But meat eaters were still dangerous to young Brachiosaurus.

WHO WAS BIGGEST?

BRACHIOSAURUS
40 feet (12 m)

ALLOSAURUS
16 feet (4.9 m)

DEINONYCHUS
6 feet (1.8 m)

COMPSOGNATHUS
1 foot (0.3 m)

Brachiosaurus wasn't related to giraffes. But it was built like them.

CHAPTER 4

New DISCOVERIES

Sometimes people make mistakes. In 1914, a scientist thought he found Brachiosaurus fossils in Tanzania. He was wrong though. They were from a different dinosaur, Giraffatitan. Now scientists know that Brachiosaurus lived in North America.

More Questions

Scientists have learned a lot about Brachiosaurus. But they don't know everything. They still wonder what color Brachiosaurus was. Did it lay eggs in a circle? It might have made it harder to crush the eggs. Did it take care of its young? More discoveries can still be made.

Brachiosaurus teeth

dinosaur tracks

GLOSSARY

compete (kuhm-PEET)—to try to get or win something that someone or something else is trying to get or win

cycad (SY-kuhd)—a plant like a palm with a thick woody trunk and stiff leaves growing from the center

fern (FURN)—a type of plant that has large, delicate leaves and no flowers

fossil (FAH-sul)—the remains or traces of plants and animals that are preserved as rock

ginkgo (GING-koh)—a large tree that has fan-shaped leaves

herd (HURD)—a group of animals

strip (STRIP)—to remove a covering or surface layer from something

LEARN MORE

BOOKS

Sabelko, Rebecca. *Brachiosaurus.* The World of Dinosaurs. Minneapolis: Bellwether Media, Inc., 2022.

Taylor, Charlotte. *Digging Up Dinosaur Fossils.* Digging Deep into Fossils. New York: Enslow Publishing, 2022.

Weakland, Mark. *Long-Necked Dinosaurs: Ranking Their Speed, Strength, and Smarts.* Dinosaurs by Design. Mankato, Minn.: Black Rabbit Books, 2020.

WEBSITES

Brachiosaurus
kids.nationalgeographic.com/animals/prehistoric/facts/brachiosaurus

Brachiosaurus
www.dkfindout.com/us/dinosaurs-and-prehistoric-life/dinosaurs/brachiosaurus/

Brachiosaurus Facts for Kids, Students, and Adults—Information and Pictures
activewild.com/brachiosaurus-facts-pictures-information/

INDEX

D
diet, 7, 20–21, 23

discoveries, 16, 28

F
features, 7, 10–11, 20

fossils, 16, 18, 27

H
habitat, 12, 27

herds, 8,

M
movement, 8

N
name, 7, 16

P
predators, 24

S
size, 4, 8–9, 25

T
time period, 12, 14–15